# GO GET IT GIRL

TRUE STORIES RADIO

GALERON CONSULTING

# INTRODUCTION

"Go Get It, Girl"

Awaken your potential, stoke the fire within, and embark on a life-changing journey of personal and professional growth with "Go Get It, Girl." This book, brimming with wisdom, insight, and practical advice, is your definitive guide to realizing your dreams and becoming the best version of yourself.

"Go Get It, Girl" draws on the author's extensive experience as a life coach, consultant, motivational speaker, and online course creator, providing readers with a compelling roadmap towards success. The book is divided into five transformative chapters, each focusing on an essential aspect of self-improvement and empowerment.

The journey begins with the process of self-discovery, helping you unearth your true purpose and potential. It then navigates through the importance of resilience, persistence, and goal-setting. The narrative delves into holistic well-being, discussing the nourishment of your mind, body, and soul. The book then shifts to practical strategies on personal branding, relationship building, social media utilization, and financial mastery, effectively enabling you to start building your own empire.

The concluding chapter emphasizes the significance of embracing the journey itself—celebrating achievements, maintaining a practice of reflection and gratitude, and learning to savor each moment.

"Go Get It, Girl" is more than a self-help book—it's a call to action. This book urges you to seize the reins of your life and gallop towards your dreams. Each page is a testament to the power of determination, urging you to rise, shine, and conquer. This book is your clarion call to action - so go get it, girl!

# PREFACE

The preface of "Go Get It, Girl" provides an overview of the inspiration behind this transformative guide. The author shares his personal journey as a life coach, consultant, and motivational speaker, describing how he's used his experiences to guide others on their journeys of personal and professional growth.

# COPYRIGHT

Copyright © GO GET IT GIRL by FLYNN EAMON

All rights reserved.

No portion of this book may be reproduced in any form without written permission from the publisher or author, except as permitted by U.S. copyright law.

# Contents

| | |
|---|---|
| About the Author | IX |
| Epigraph | X |
| Dedication | XI |
| 1. Chapter 1: Igniting the Flame | 1 |
| Discovering Your Purpose | 2 |
| Embracing Your Identity | 6 |
| The Fire Within | 10 |
| Sowing the Seeds of Success | 13 |
| 2. Chapter 2: Embrace the Hustle | 16 |
| Building Resilience | 17 |
| The Art of Persistence | 22 |
| Prioritizing Your Goals | 25 |
| The Power of Consistency | 28 |
| 3. Chapter 3: Nurturing Your Mind, Body, and Soul | 31 |
| Cultivating a Positive Mindset | 32 |
| The Role of Physical Well-being | 35 |
| Feeding Your Soul | 38 |
| Emotional Intelligence and Success | 41 |

4. Chapter 4: Building Your Empire — 44
Cultivating Your Personal Brand — 45
Networking and Relationship Buildings — 47
The Power of Social Media — 50
Financial Mastery — 53
5. Chapter 5: Celebrating the Journey — 56
Embracing Your Achievements — 57
Reflecting and Adjusting — 60
The Art of Gratitude — 62
Savoring the Moment — 64

# ABOUT THE AUTHOR

The author of "Go Get It, Girl" is an experienced life coach, consultant, and motivational speaker with a passion for helping others achieve their dreams. He has dedicated his career to empowering women in their personal and professional lives.

"Do not wait for leaders; do it alone, person to person." - Mother Teresa

This book is dedicated to all the women out there who are ready to realize their dreams, embrace their potential, and take the world by storm. You are unstoppable.

# Chapter 1: Igniting the Flame

# Discovering Your Purpose

In my years as a life coach, consultant, and motivational speaker, one truth consistently stands out - nothing propels us more powerfully towards our dreams than understanding our purpose.

Let's take a look at the life of Amelia, a client I once worked with. She was a high-performing executive, with commendations and accolades galore. On paper, Amelia had it all, but beneath the veneer of success, she was adrift, struggling with a gnawing sense of emptiness. Despite her accomplishments, she felt like she was just going through the motions. Like many others, Amelia was seeking more than success; she was seeking purpose.

Discovering our purpose isn't about picking a random passion and hoping it works out. It's a deep, introspective journey of self-discovery, about aligning our lives with the values that are most important to us. It's about finding that unique intersection of our skills, interests, and opportunities, where we feel most alive and impactful. It's about understanding who we are, what we care about, and how we can make a difference.

For those who are just beginning this journey, it can be overwhelming. Where do we start? What steps do we take? The key is to start with self-reflection. It's the simple act of turning our gaze inward, examining our thoughts, feelings, beliefs, and motivations. Self-reflection isn't about judging ourselves or comparing our journey to others. It's about understanding ourselves better so we can make decisions that align with our true selves.

You might be wondering, how exactly do we practice self-reflection? There are numerous tools and techniques, but journaling is a particularly effective method. It provides a private, judgment-free space where we can express our thoughts and feelings freely. It helps us see patterns, recognize triggers, and gain insight into our behaviors. Try setting aside 15-20 minutes a day to journal. Write about your day, your feelings, your dreams, and your fears. Write about the moments you felt most alive, and the moments you felt lost. Don't censor yourself, and don't worry about grammar or punctuation. This journal is for you, and you alone.

As we engage in self-reflection, we'll begin to see common threads - values, interests, and causes that stir our hearts. These are clues to our purpose. To further crystallize these insights, we can use another tool - the purpose statement. It's a succinct expression of what we stand for, what we want to achieve, and how we want to make a difference. Crafting a purpose statement can give us a clear sense of direction and keep us grounded when life gets chaotic.

Here's a simple template to get you started: "I exist to (how you want to impact the world) by (actions you'll take) because (why it's important to you)." Don't worry about getting it perfect the first time. Your purpose statement is a living document that will evolve as you grow and learn.

Having a purpose, however, doesn't mean we won't face obstacles or doubts. I remember a time in my own journey when, despite having a clear sense of purpose, I was paralyzed with fear and self-doubt. I was about to launch my first online course, and I was terrified. What if no one signed up? What if people hated it? What if I failed? But as I grappled with my fear, I remembered my purpose - to inspire and empower others to realize their dreams. This reminder gave me the courage to take the leap, despite my fear.

Understanding our purpose can also help us make difficult decisions. Let's take

the example of Robert, a bright young software engineer who I once counseled. He was in a dilemma, torn between a lucrative job offer from a multinational corporation and a risky opportunity to join a nonprofit organization that aimed to use technology for social impact. While the corporate job offered financial security, the nonprofit resonated with Robert's deep-seated desire to use his skills for a larger purpose. Recalling his purpose statement, "I exist to leverage technology to uplift and empower marginalized communities," made the decision clear. Robert chose the nonprofit, trading in some financial gain for a career that fulfilled him deeply.

Our purpose can guide us, but it's also important to remember that discovering it doesn't happen overnight. It's a journey, filled with exploration, reflection, and even a few wrong turns. But with every step, every stumble, we learn more about ourselves and move closer to a life that reflects who we truly are.

Moreover, having a purpose doesn't mean we have to stick to a rigid path. In fact, flexibility is key. Our interests, our circumstances, and the world around us are constantly changing, and our purpose can evolve with them. Flexibility allows us to adapt and grow, to find new ways of living our purpose that align with who we are becoming.

It's also important to periodically check in with ourselves, to reflect on our journey and reassess our direction. Are we living in alignment with our purpose? Are we making decisions that reflect our values? Are we honoring our interests and passions? Regular reflection can keep us grounded in our purpose and help us course-correct when necessary.

To deepen your understanding of purpose and its power, I recommend "The Power of Purpose" by Richard Leider. Leider, a renowned coach, articulates the profound impact of living a purpose-driven life and offers practical tools for discovering and articulating your own purpose. Additionally, the TED Talk "There's more to life than being happy" by Emily Esfahani Smith is a thought-provoking exploration of how purpose, more than fleeting happiness, brings true fulfillment.

In conclusion, discovering our purpose is one of the most transformative journeys we can undertake. It involves self-reflection, honesty, courage, and patience. But the reward - a life lived in alignment with who we truly are - is immeasurable. As you embark on this journey, remember, you are not alone. As your coach, I am here to guide and support you every step of the way. So, let's ignite the flame of your potential and discover the purpose that lies within you. Because, girl, the world needs your unique gifts, your unique passion, your unique purpose. So go get it!

# Embracing Your Identity

As a life coach, consultant, and motivational speaker, I've had the privilege of guiding many individuals on their personal and professional journeys. An integral part of this journey, often overlooked, is understanding and embracing one's unique identity. Let's unpack this powerful process and explore how it can fuel your growth and success.

In my early career, I encountered an aspiring entrepreneur named Lisa. Lisa had a promising idea for a sustainable fashion line, but she was hesitant to get started. She believed her identity as a woman and a person of color might hinder her success in the male-dominated business world. Together, we embarked on a journey of self-discovery, where Lisa learned not to see her identity as an obstacle but rather as an asset.

Your identity is the sum total of your experiences, beliefs, values, and traits that make you unique. It's not merely about how the world sees you, but about how you see yourself. It forms the lens through which you understand the world, shaping your thoughts, decisions, and actions. In essence, your identity is the cornerstone of your existence.

Becoming aware of your identity is a voyage inward. It requires self-reflection, an honest examination of your experiences, values, and beliefs. You might ask, "What experiences have shaped me? What values are closest to my heart? What parts of my identity am I most proud of?" Journaling can be a powerful tool for this introspection. By regularly writing down your thoughts, feelings, and experiences, you can uncover patterns and themes that offer insights into your identity.

Understanding your identity is just the first step. The real magic happens when you embrace it. Embracing your identity means honoring all aspects of who you are, including your strengths, flaws, and everything in between. It means owning your story, your experiences, and your journey. It means recognizing the power and potential that lie within your unique self.

To embrace her identity, Lisa had to confront societal stereotypes and her own self-doubt. She had to understand that being a woman and a person of color did not diminish her potential but rather enriched it. Her unique experiences and perspectives allowed her to approach business in a unique way, to connect with a diverse audience, and to build a brand that was genuine and relatable.

Embracing your identity also enables authenticity. In a world that often encourages conformity, authenticity is a breath of fresh air. It's about being true to who you are, expressing your thoughts and feelings honestly, and living in alignment with your values. Authenticity attracts people and opportunities that resonate with your true self, fostering deeper connections and more fulfilling experiences.

Cultivating authenticity involves self-awareness, courage, and integrity. It requires self-awareness to understand who you are, courage to express your true self, and integrity to live in alignment with your values. To foster authenticity, I often recommend an exercise called 'The Authenticity Check'. At the end of each day, reflect on your interactions and decisions. Ask yourself, "Did I act in alignment with my true self? Did I express my thoughts and feelings honestly? Did I honor my values?" This regular check can help you stay true to your authentic self.

However, embracing your identity doesn't mean becoming rigid or complacent. Your identity is dynamic, evolving as you grow and learn. It's important to remain open to new experiences, ideas, and perspectives that can expand and enrich your understanding of yourself.

Just as a river's course can change over time, your identity can shift and adapt. It's essential to periodically reflect on your identity and make adjustments as needed. This can be as simple as taking a few minutes each day to reflect on your experiences and how they've influenced your sense of self. Ask yourself, "Am I growing in a way that aligns with my authentic self? Are there new aspects of my identity that I need to embrace?"

Moreover, embracing your identity is not an invitation to narcissism or self-centeredness. It's about understanding and accepting who you are while also acknowledging and respecting the unique identities of others. It's about fostering empathy, celebrating diversity, and building a more inclusive and compassionate world.

If you're interested in further exploring the concept of identity, I highly recommend the book "The Gifts of Imperfection" by Brené Brown. Brown's insightful and compassionate approach to embracing our authentic selves is both empowering and transformative. Additionally, the TED Talk "The Power of Vulnerability" by the same author provides profound insights into how embracing our vulnerabilities, a core aspect of our identity, can lead to a more fulfilling and connected life.

In conclusion, understanding and embracing your identity is a transformative journey of self-discovery and self-love. It's about owning your story, cherishing your uniqueness, and living authentically. It's about recognizing the power and potential that lie within your unique self. As you embark on this journey, remember, there is no one else like you in this world. You are uniquely equipped to make a difference in a way that no one else can. So embrace your identity, own your power, and let your authentic light shine. Because, girl, when you shine, the world shines with you. So go get it!

# The Fire Within

As an experienced life coach and motivational speaker, I've noticed that the most successful individuals share a common trait: a burning desire to realize their potential and make their mark on the world. I refer to this potent force as "the fire within," and in this section, we will explore ways to ignite and harness this inner fire.

Many years ago, I met Jason, a talented artist struggling to make ends meet. Jason's extraordinary talent was evident in his vivid and expressive pieces, but his paintings remained unsold, stacked high in his small studio. Yet, when I looked into Jason's eyes, I saw a spark—a deep-rooted desire to share his artistic vision with the world. It was this fire within that ultimately transformed his passion into a thriving art career.

We all have this inner fire, a blend of passion, ambition, and resilience. This flame represents our deepest desires and aspirations, the goals we are passionate about achieving, and the difference we yearn to make in the world. Yet, many of us stifle this flame, allowing self-doubt, fear, or complacency to overshadow our true potential.

Igniting this inner fire requires self-discovery. We must delve deep within ourselves, exploring our interests, passions, values, and dreams. This process requires courage and honesty, but the reward is a clear vision of what we truly desire and the motivation to pursue it relentlessly.

One of the most powerful tools for this self-discovery is visualization. Visualization involves mentally picturing your desired future, immersing yourself in the feelings, sights, and sounds associated with your goals. By regularly practicing visualization, you can stoke your inner fire and keep your ambitions alive.

Yet, simply igniting the fire is not enough. We must also harness its warmth and light, using it to fuel our journey towards our goals. This requires a clear plan of action—a roadmap that outlines the steps needed to transform our fiery desires into tangible realities.

Creating this plan involves setting clear, achievable goals, breaking them down into manageable tasks, and tracking our progress. It's important to celebrate our victories, no matter how small, as these moments of success fan the flames of our inner fire.

Yet, the path to our goals is seldom linear. It's filled with twists and turns, obstacles, and setbacks. In such times, our inner fire becomes our beacon of hope, reminding us of our potential and motivating us to push forward. It's this resilience—the ability to bounce back from adversity—that truly sets successful individuals apart.

Resilience is not an innate trait; it's a skill that can be cultivated. One way to foster resilience is through mindfulness—a practice of staying present and engaged in the current moment. Mindfulness allows us to navigate challenges with a calm and focused mind, reducing stress and enhancing our problem-solving abilities.

For further exploration of resilience and mindfulness, I highly recommend "Rising Strong" by Brené Brown. Brown's groundbreaking research on vulnerability and resilience offers valuable insights and practical tools to navigate life's ups and downs. Additionally, the app "Headspace" offers guided mindfulness exercises to help cultivate a calm and resilient mind.

Remember, your inner fire is a reflection of your unique potential. It's your personal compass, guiding you towards your goals and aspirations. It's your source of motivation, resilience, and hope. So, keep your flame burning bright. Cherish your dreams, honor your passions, and commit to your journey. Because, girl, when you ignite the fire within, there's nothing you can't achieve. So go get it!

# Sowing the Seeds of Success

Have you ever wondered why some individuals appear to thrive in the face of adversity, using their challenges as stepping stones towards success, while others falter and crumble? From my years of experience as a life coach, consultant, and motivational speaker, I can tell you that the answer lies in the seeds we choose to sow.

Consider the story of Sarah, a client of mine who came to me, feeling defeated by life's challenges. Sarah had dreams, aspirations just like anyone else, but the obstacles she faced had left her feeling overwhelmed and hopeless. Despite her current situation, Sarah possessed a critical element for success: the desire for change. This desire was her seed, a tiny speck of potential that could grow into something significant if nurtured appropriately.

Sowing the seeds of success begins with identifying our desires, our dreams, and our goals. It's about understanding where we are, acknowledging where we want to be, and mapping out how to get there. This process requires introspection and self-awareness, characteristics that we'll nurture as we progress through this book.

Having clear, well-defined goals acts as our compass, guiding us on our journey towards success. Yet, merely having these goals is not enough. We need to plant these seeds of ambition deep within our subconscious minds, watering them with consistent action, patience, and perseverance.

A valuable tool in this planting process is affirmations. Positive, empowering affirmations act as fertilizer, reinforcing our belief in our goals and our ability to achieve them. When we consistently affirm our ambitions, we cultivate a mindset of success, reinforcing our resilience and determination.

Yet, it's not just about sowing the right seeds. We must also tend to our garden of dreams, ensuring that the soil—our subconscious mind—is healthy and receptive. This requires us to uproot any weeds of self-doubt, fear, or negativity that could choke our aspirations. It involves nurturing a positive, growth-oriented mindset, one that views challenges as opportunities for growth rather than obstacles.

A helpful technique for maintaining this positive mindset is gratitude. Regularly expressing gratitude for our blessings—be it our talents, our opportunities, or the support we receive—can shift our focus from what we lack to what we possess. This shift in perspective can significantly enhance our motivation, resilience, and overall well-being.

Along our journey towards success, we must also practice patience. Just as a seed doesn't sprout overnight, our goals will take time to manifest. It's during these waiting periods that our commitment is truly tested. Remember, it's not about the speed at which we reach our goals, but the growth we experience along the way.

For more on patience and perseverance, I recommend reading "Grit: The Power of Passion and Perseverance" by Angela Duckworth. This enlightening book delves into the science behind grit—a combination of passion and perseverance—and provides practical strategies to cultivate it.

Lastly, as we tend to our seeds of success, we must remember that our growth impacts those around us. As we evolve, we influence others, inspiring them to sow their seeds of success. So, by pursuing our dreams, we're not just transforming our lives; we're contributing to a more empowered, purpose-driven world.

In summary, success isn't an overnight phenomenon. It's a journey, a process of sowing, tending, and harvesting. It's about planting the seeds of your dreams, nurturing them with consistent action and a positive mindset, and patiently waiting as your garden of aspirations comes to life. Remember, your dreams are worth the effort. So, go get it, girl! Let's start sowing the seeds of your success. (Word Count

# Chapter 2: Embrace the Hustle

# BUILDING RESILIENCE

Resilience, a cornerstone of personal success and fulfillment, is the ability to adapt and bounce back when things don't go as planned. It is a mental reservoir of strength that can be drawn upon in times of need. As a seasoned life coach, consultant, and motivational speaker, I've observed that those who possess this quality are not just survivors; they are capable of thriving, even under the most challenging circumstances.

For instance, consider the story of Linda, a client of mine who encountered numerous obstacles on her journey to become a successful entrepreneur. Linda faced everything from financial setbacks to personal losses, yet she persevered. Her resilience didn't prevent her from experiencing these hardships, but it did empower her to navigate through them and emerge stronger.

So, how can you cultivate such resilience?

It starts with understanding and accepting that challenges and setbacks are a part of life. None of us are immune to adversity. The difference lies in how we perceive and respond to these hardships. By viewing challenges as opportunities for growth and learning, we begin to cultivate a resilient mindset.

Self-belief is another crucial aspect of resilience. Believe in your abilities, your potential, and your capacity to overcome adversity. Our beliefs have a significant influence on our actions and our responses to different situations. Positive self-belief encourages us to take risks, push our boundaries, and bounce back after setbacks.

Keeping the company of positive and supportive individuals can also help build resilience. Our social environment influences our attitudes and behaviors. Surrounding yourself with positive, resilient individuals can foster a similar attitude in you, helping you to remain motivated and focused during difficult times.

Self-care is a critical element often overlooked in the hustle. To continue moving forward, it's essential to replenish your physical, mental, and emotional energy. Establishing regular self-care practices—like maintaining a healthy diet, getting regular exercise, and ensuring adequate sleep—can significantly boost your resilience.

Mindfulness and meditation are also powerful tools for cultivating resilience. These practices help to reduce stress, increase self-awareness, and enhance emotional regulation—factors that contribute significantly to resilience. There are numerous resources available for learning mindfulness and meditation, one of which is the book "Wherever You Go, There You Are: Mindfulness Meditation in Everyday Life" by Jon Kabat-Zinn.

Another important part of building resilience is to remember that it's okay to seek help when needed. Seeking support, whether from a trusted friend, a mentor, or a professional, is not a sign of weakness; instead, it is a testament to your strength and your commitment to personal growth.

Regularly reviewing and reflecting on your progress can also enhance your resilience. Celebrate your achievements, no matter how small they might seem, and learn from your setbacks. These practices can strengthen your belief in your abilities and boost your motivation to keep going.

Lastly, maintaining a sense of humor can do wonders for your resilience. Laughter and positivity can lighten your mood, reduce stress, and help you maintain perspective in challenging situations. So, remember to find joy and laughter, even in the hustle.

In essence, building resilience is about cultivating a positive and realistic mindset, believing in your abilities, taking care of your well-being, learning from your experiences, and being unafraid to seek help when needed. It's not an overnight process, but a lifelong journey of personal growth and learning. As you embrace the hustle, remember to nurture your resilience, for it is the fire that will keep you going, no matter what.

Continue to sow the seeds of resilience in the garden of your life, and you will be astounded by the strength and tenacity that blooms. Embrace the hustle, my friend, because it is the journey, the learning, and the growth that truly defines success, not just the destination.

To cultivate resilience, it is crucial to practice self-compassion. Too often, we are our own harshest critics. We scrutinize our failures, mistakes, or inadequacies, berating ourselves for our perceived shortcomings. This self-criticism can drain our resilience, leaving us feeling defeated and despondent. In contrast, when we treat ourselves with kindness and understanding—when we extend to ourselves the same compassion we would to a dear friend—we bolster our resilience.

Dr. Kristin Neff, a pioneering researcher in the field of self-compassion, provides profound insights into this practice in her book "Self-Compassion: The Proven Power of Being Kind to Yourself". This resource can serve as a helpful guide as you embark on your journey of cultivating self-compassion, a crucial component of resilience.

Remember, resilience does not mean denying or suppressing your feelings. Experiencing emotions—both positive and negative—is part of the human experience.

Allow yourself to feel these emotions without judgment. Acknowledge your feelings, understand them, and then channel them in a manner that supports your growth and well-being. Resilience involves maintaining your equilibrium and moving forward, despite experiencing setbacks or negative emotions.

A powerful technique that can help in this regard is journaling. Writing about your thoughts, feelings, and experiences can provide emotional catharsis, enhance self-understanding, and promote problem-solving. It serves as a medium for you to express your emotions freely, thereby supporting emotional regulation—a vital aspect of resilience.

Setting healthy boundaries is another crucial element in building resilience. Recognize your limits and learn to say 'no' when necessary. Overextending yourself—whether physically, emotionally, or mentally—can deplete your resilience, leaving you feeling overwhelmed and exhausted. Protect your time and energy by setting clear boundaries and honoring them.

Resilience, much like a muscle, strengthens with regular practice. Each challenge, each setback presents an opportunity for you to practice and strengthen your resilience. With each hurdle you overcome, you'll find yourself growing more confident and capable. It is this resilience that will empower you to embrace the hustle and thrive, irrespective of the challenges that come your way.

In the words of renowned author Elizabeth Edwards, "Resilience is accepting your new reality, even if it's less good than the one you had before. You can fight it, you can do nothing but scream about what you've lost, or you can accept that and try to put together something that's good."

The road to resilience is not a straight, easy path, but rather a winding trail with ups and downs. It takes time, patience, and commitment. It requires you to stretch your capabilities and step outside your comfort zone. But as you journey along this path, you'll discover a strength within you that is greater than any challenge or adversity.

Remember, resilience isn't about avoiding the storm but learning to dance in the rain. So, go ahead, put on your dancing shoes, and embrace the hustle. After all, it's through the hustle that you'll discover your true potential, your resilience, and your ability to succeed against all odds.

# The Art of Persistence

The Art of Persistence, let's now explore an attribute often misconstrued as stubbornness, but in fact, it is the powerful trait that can turn your dreams into reality - persistence. As Calvin Coolidge once aptly said, "Nothing in the world can take the place of persistence. Talent will not; nothing is more common than unsuccessful men with talent. Genius will not; unrewarded genius is almost a proverb. Education will not; the world is full of educated derelicts. Persistence and determination alone are omnipotent."

Persistence, like any art, is a craft that you can learn, master, and utilize to shape your destiny. The key is to remember that persistence is not about doing the same thing repetitively and expecting different results. Instead, it's about constantly learning, adapting, and finding new ways to approach the problems at hand until you finally reach your goal. This section, dear reader, aims to guide you in mastering this art, this dance of persistence, so let's begin.

An inevitable part of life's journey is experiencing setbacks. What separates those who achieve their dreams from those who do not is not the absence of obstacles but the ability to persist in the face of them. The willingness to get up every time life knocks you down, dust yourself off, learn from the experience, and move forward with renewed determination is what defines persistence. It's this spirit that allows one to turn failure into fuel and challenges into stepping stones, ultimately leading to success.

As a life coach, I have seen firsthand the transformative power of persistence in my clients' lives. One particular example that comes to mind is of a young woman named Lucy. After numerous failed attempts to launch her own business, Lucy was on the brink of giving up. However, she chose to persevere. With each failure, she learned, adapted, and grew. It was her persistence that eventually led her to establish a successful business that is now thriving. Her story serves as a testament to the power of persistence.

Understanding that failure is not the opposite of success, but a part of the process is crucial. A helpful resource in reshaping your perspective towards failure is the book "Failing Forward: Turning Mistakes into Stepping Stones for Success" by John C. Maxwell. This book provides valuable insights into how one can leverage failures as opportunities for growth and learning, a key aspect of persistence.

To foster persistence, setting clear, achievable goals is paramount. Start with small, manageable goals, and gradually work your way up to larger, more challenging ones. Each achievement, no matter how small, will boost your confidence and reinforce your persistence.

A practical tool that can aid in goal setting is the SMART framework, an acronym for Specific, Measurable, Achievable, Relevant, and Time-bound. This framework provides a structured and effective approach to setting goals, thereby promoting persistence.

Practice makes perfect, and this is especially true when it comes to the art of persistence. Make it a habit to step outside your comfort zone regularly. Engage in tasks and activities that challenge you. Over time, you'll find your capacity for persistence expanding, enabling you to tackle bigger and more daunting challenges.

Meditation and mindfulness can also bolster your ability to persist. They can help you stay focused and maintain your composure in the face of adversity. Apps like

Headspace and Calm offer guided meditations that can help you cultivate these skills.

Just as a river carves a path through a mountain, not through its power, but through its persistence, you too can carve a path to your dreams through the power of persistence. Embrace the hustle, dear reader, and let your persistent spirit lead you to success.

# PRIORITIZING YOUR GOALS

We continue our journey to success with an exploration of goal-setting, but not just any goal-setting. We delve into the art of setting your objectives in order of importance, an essential factor for efficient productivity and achievement. This chapter's focus revolves around the theory and the practicality behind the ranking of your dreams and ambitions.

Life is a vast ocean of possibilities. We are, more often than not, bombarded with an overwhelming number of options and potential paths, making it challenging to determine where we should direct our energy. It's like trying to juggle an array of different balls, and each ball represents a goal. If we try to juggle them all without setting a priority, we're likely to drop them all. That's where prioritization comes into play.

Prioritizing your goals is not about discarding some dreams in favor of others. Instead, it's about recognizing that we cannot do everything at once. It's about understanding that success in one area can create success in another, and that it's okay to focus on one goal at a time. Prioritization equips us with the clarity to direct our efforts effectively and the ability to achieve our goals more efficiently.

As an experienced life coach, I have seen the power of prioritization work wonders in my clients' lives. A fitting example is John, a man brimming with ambition. John had a wide range of goals, from starting his own business to running a marathon. However, he was struggling to make progress in any of his objectives.

The problem was not a lack of willpower or capability but a lack of prioritization. After working together to prioritize his goals, John was able to make significant strides towards his dreams.

Through John's journey, we can understand the transformative power of goal prioritization. It enables us to focus, avoid feeling overwhelmed, and make effective use of our time and resources. It allows us to align our daily actions with our long-term vision.

To begin prioritizing your goals, list down all your objectives. Next, determine the importance of each goal, considering factors like the potential impact on your life, the effort required, and the alignment with your long-term vision. A highly recommended tool for this process is the Eisenhower Box, a simple matrix that can help you decide which goals to focus on first, which ones to schedule for later, which ones to delegate, and which ones to eliminate.

Just as with any skill, prioritizing goals requires practice. Start with small goals and gradually move to bigger ones. Remember, it's okay to re-evaluate and change your priorities as circumstances change. Flexibility is key in this process.

Mindfulness can also aid in prioritizing goals. By fostering a heightened awareness of our thoughts and feelings, mindfulness allows us to stay true to our values, helping us to prioritize goals that truly resonate with us. Apps like Headspace offer valuable resources for practicing mindfulness.

Recommended reading to delve deeper into this subject includes "Essentialism: The Disciplined Pursuit of Less" by Greg McKeown. The book offers profound insights into focusing on the essential and eliminating the rest, aligning perfectly with our topic of prioritizing goals.

Remember, the essence of prioritizing your goals is not about sacrificing some dreams for others. Instead, it's about paving a clear path towards your dreams by focusing your energy efficiently. Embrace the hustle, knowing that every step you take is a step closer to realizing your dreams.

# The Power of Consistency

This chapter is particularly special as it underlines the importance of staying consistent, which is the very backbone of success in any endeavor. You see, it's not the grand one-time actions but the small, consistent steps taken every day that lead to big results.

Every significant accomplishment in life, be it professional success, a healthy body, or nurturing relationships, is the result of consistent action. Consistency, or the commitment to doing something regularly over time, regardless of immediate outcomes, is a common trait found in every successful person you can think of.

Let's consider the example of Sarah, a client I've worked with in the past. Sarah was an aspiring writer who had the talent but couldn't manage to complete a manuscript. Her writing schedule was sporadic at best, making her progress slow and leading to frequent bouts of writer's block.

After discussing her challenges, we decided to implement a simple strategy: writing for at least one hour each day. Regardless of the number of words or the quality of the writing, the goal was to be consistent. Fast forward six months later, Sarah had completed her first manuscript and managed to secure a publishing deal. She proved that the smallest consistent action, when performed daily, could lead to grand achievements.

On the surface, consistency may seem like a simple concept, but in practice, it's one of the most challenging skills to master. However, once mastered, it can become your most potent tool in achieving success.

There are some strategies to help you build consistency. First and foremost, it's essential to set realistic goals. Make sure your daily actions are manageable and not overwhelming. Next, create a routine or a habit around your goal. For instance, if your objective is to write a book, make writing a part of your daily routine. Write at the same time every day to help it become a habit.

Another vital tool in maintaining consistency is tracking your progress. Keep a journal or use an app to document your daily actions and observe your progress. This practice allows you to see the tangible results of your consistent actions over time, providing motivation to keep going.

Also, remember to show yourself grace and flexibility. Life happens, and there will be days when you fall off the wagon. Instead of beating yourself up and quitting, show some compassion and get back on track the next day.

Consistency also requires a good deal of mental fortitude. Meditation can be a fantastic tool for developing the mental strength needed to stay consistent. The Headspace app provides various guided meditations that can help.

Consistency is not just about repetitiveness; it's about commitment, patience, and showing up even when you don't feel like it. Consistency transforms promises into habits, dreams into realities, and turns the ordinary into the extraordinary.

One of the best resources to delve deeper into this subject is the book "The Compound Effect" by Darren Hardy. The book beautifully explains how the cumulative impact of small, consistent actions can lead to massive results over time.

Remember, embracing the hustle isn't about monumental, one-off efforts but about showing up consistently, putting in the work, and moving steadily towards your goals. So, keep showing up, keep putting in the work, and let the power of consistency guide you to your desired success.

# Chapter 3: Nurturing Your Mind, Body, and Soul

# Cultivating a Positive Mindset

As we delve into Chapter 3, Section 3.1: "Cultivating a Positive Mindset," we embark on a journey that highlights the importance of fostering positivity within ourselves. As a life coach, consultant, and motivational speaker, I've witnessed how one's mindset can either facilitate or hinder growth. So let's explore how we can cultivate a positive mindset to bring about powerful transformations.

The human mind is a fertile ground where seeds of thought, both positive and negative, can take root and flourish. The thoughts we nurture and the mental attitudes we foster significantly influence our perception of the world and our experiences. A positive mindset is a powerful tool that can illuminate our path, fuel our motivation, and encourage resilience amid adversity.

I recall the story of a client, David, who was struggling with a career rut. He was filled with negativity, often expressing that he was too old to change careers or learn new skills. After several sessions, we decided to focus on shifting his mindset from negativity to positivity.

One tool we used was positive affirmations. David began his day by saying affirmations such as, "I am capable of learning and growing" and "I am not too old to embrace change." This simple practice started shifting his mindset. Over time, David embraced learning and eventually transitioned into a new career he found rewarding. David's story is a testament to the power of a positive mindset.

How can we foster a positive mindset? First, recognize the power of your thoughts and make a conscious effort to feed your mind positive, empowering thoughts. Practice self-awareness, become mindful of your thought patterns, and challenge negative or limiting beliefs.

Next, practice gratitude. Make it a habit to appreciate what you have, no matter how small. Gratitude can shift your focus from what's lacking to what's abundant in your life, fostering positivity. Try to maintain a gratitude journal where you jot down a few things you're grateful for each day.

Moreover, surround yourself with positivity. This includes people, environments, and activities that inspire, uplift, and encourage you. Avoid unnecessary negativity, whether it's people who constantly complain or news that stirs up fear and anxiety.

Self-care is another essential component of a positive mindset. Taking care of your physical health, eating a balanced diet, getting regular exercise, and ensuring adequate sleep can significantly impact your mental state.

Meditation and mindfulness can also be incredibly beneficial. Apps like Calm and Headspace offer a variety of guided meditations aimed at fostering positivity.

Finally, remember to practice patience and persistence. Cultivating a positive mindset isn't an overnight process; it takes time, so be patient with yourself.

For further reading, I'd recommend "The Power of Positive Thinking" by Norman Vincent Peale. This classic book provides practical instructions to energize your life and give you the initiative needed to carry out your ambitions and hopes.

Your mind is a garden. When you cultivate positivity, you're planting the seeds of success, happiness, and well-being. You're preparing the ground for growth, resilience, and a fulfilling life. So, let's start planting those positive seeds today and reap the beautiful harvest in all aspects of our lives tomorrow.

This journey is not just about transforming your mindset, but also nurturing your mind, body, and soul. Remember, a positive mindset isn't the absence of negative thoughts, but choosing positivity in the face of adversity. You have the power within you to cultivate a positive mindset, so make that choice today, and every day henceforth.

# The Role of Physical Well-being

In Section 3.2, "The Role of Physical Well-being," we are going to examine the interconnectedness of the mind and body, and why taking care of our physical health is vital to our overall wellness. We often overlook our physical health in the race to achieve our goals and dreams. However, having experienced many ups and downs in life and having coached numerous individuals over the years, I have come to understand that our physical well-being plays an instrumental role in our overall success and happiness.

Visualize your body as a vehicle. To reach your desired destination, the vehicle needs to be well-maintained, fueled, and taken care of. The same applies to your body. You cannot reach the pinnacle of your potential if your body isn't well-nurtured.

During my early days as a consultant, I met a young entrepreneur named Lisa. Lisa was passionate, talented, and driven. She was running a successful startup and was dedicated to her work. However, her dedication came at the expense of her health. Long hours at the office, skipped meals, lack of physical activity, and insufficient sleep began taking a toll on her. Eventually, she experienced burnout, her productivity declined, and her business began to suffer.

Working with Lisa, we developed a comprehensive plan that focused not only on her business goals but also her physical health. We incorporated regular exercise, a balanced diet, and adequate sleep into her routine. We also introduced stress management techniques such as yoga and meditation.

Over time, Lisa started feeling more energetic, her focus improved, and she was better equipped to handle the challenges of her business. Her business regained its momentum, and she learned a valuable lesson about the role of physical well-being in success.

Now, let's look at the key elements of physical well-being and how you can incorporate them into your life.

First and foremost, regular exercise is essential. Exercise isn't only about maintaining a healthy weight or physique; it's about keeping your body active and agile. It helps release endorphins, the body's natural mood boosters. Start with simple exercises such as walking, jogging, or cycling, and gradually move on to more strenuous activities as your fitness improves.

Next, focus on your diet. Remember, you are what you eat. Your diet should be balanced, rich in fruits, vegetables, lean proteins, and whole grains. Avoid processed foods, excessive sugar, and unhealthy fats. Stay well-hydrated by drinking enough water throughout the day.

Sleep is another vital aspect of physical well-being. Ensure you get at least 7-8 hours of sleep every night. Lack of sleep can affect your mood, productivity, and overall health.

Lastly, learn to manage stress. Chronic stress can lead to various health issues, including heart disease, high blood pressure, and mental health disorders. Incorporate stress management techniques such as yoga, meditation, or deep-breathing exercises into your routine.

For further reading on the subject, I recommend the book "Eat, Move, Sleep: How Small Choices Lead to Big Changes" by Tom Rath. It offers a holistic approach to physical well-being and provides actionable strategies for a healthier lifestyle.

Remember, your body is the temple of your soul, and taking care of it is not a luxury but a necessity. Prioritizing your physical well-being is not an act of self-indulgence but self-respect. So, respect your body, nurture it, and watch it lead you towards the path of success and fulfillment.

# FEEDING YOUR SOUL

As we journey into the third section of Chapter 3, "Feeding Your Soul," we'll explore how to nourish the often-neglected aspect of our being, the soul. This section is not about religion or spirituality, though those can certainly be avenues for feeding your soul if they resonate with you. It's about recognizing the innate need we all have for connection, meaning, and peace, and finding ways to fulfill these needs in our everyday lives.

If we consider our lives as a grand tapestry, the mind and body are the warp and weft, the vertical and horizontal threads that form the structure of the fabric. The soul, however, is the pattern that emerges, the beauty that gives the tapestry meaning. Nourishing our soul, therefore, is about enhancing this pattern, adding vibrancy and depth to our lives.

Throughout my life, I've found that the most profound moments of soul-nourishment come when we align our actions with our values, passions, and purpose. I recall a client of mine, Daniel. He was a highly successful executive, yet he confessed to feeling a sense of emptiness. Despite having achieved significant professional success, Daniel felt as though something was missing.

Working together, we unearthed that Daniel had a deep-rooted passion for music and an unfulfilled dream of learning to play the guitar. He had let this dream fall by the wayside in the pursuit of his career. Encouraging Daniel to feed his soul, we created a plan for him to start taking guitar lessons. Within a few months, Daniel reported feeling more fulfilled and less stressed. Playing the guitar had become a form of meditation for him, a way to unwind, express his feelings, and connect with a part of himself he had neglected for years.

Feeding your soul is deeply personal and different for everyone. It could be a walk in nature, reading a book, volunteering, practicing yoga, creating art, or simply spending time with loved ones. The key is to find activities that bring you joy, peace, and a sense of connection.

A practical exercise that can help is to create a "Soul-Nourishment List." Write down all the activities that you find fulfilling and make you lose track of time. Prioritize these activities in your daily life. Remember, it's not about finding large chunks of time; even a few minutes each day can make a big difference.

Importantly, feeding your soul requires you to be present. In the words of the renowned spiritual teacher Eckhart Tolle, "Realize deeply that the present moment is all you have. Make the NOW the primary focus of your life." Practice mindfulness to fully immerse yourself in whatever you're doing.

Furthermore, maintain flexibility. What feeds your soul today may not do the same a few years from now. As you evolve, your needs may change, so be open to exploring new avenues of soul nourishment.

For further insights, I recommend "The Power of Now: A Guide to Spiritual Enlightenment" by Eckhart Tolle. This book provides practical guidance on attaining peace and fulfillment in the present moment, which is crucial for feeding your soul.

In conclusion, to truly nurture your mind, body, and soul, don't neglect the part of you that craves meaning, connection, and joy. Make time for activities that feed your soul and enable you to align with your true essence. As you embark on this journey, remember that it is the quality, not the quantity, of time spent that matters. Just a few moments of soulful living each day can significantly enhance your overall well-being and quality of life.

# Emotional Intelligence and Success

Welcome to Section 3.4, "Emotional Intelligence and Success". In this part of our journey, we delve into the realm of emotional intelligence – the ability to understand, use, and manage our own emotions in positive ways, and to understand and influence the emotions of others. Emotional intelligence is as critical, if not more so, to success as intellectual ability, and in this section, we'll explore why that's the case and how you can cultivate your own emotional intelligence.

Let's start by imagining a situation that many of us can relate to. You're in a meeting at work, and your colleague proposes a plan you vehemently disagree with. Your gut reaction might be to immediately argue against the plan. But instead, you pause, taking a moment to understand why your colleague thinks this is the best course of action. You manage your initial emotional reaction, present your counterpoints respectfully, and listen to your colleague's responses with an open mind. This is emotional intelligence in action – being aware of, controlling, and expressing your emotions and handling interpersonal relationships judiciously and empathetically.

In my years as a life coach, I've found that people with high emotional intelligence tend to have stronger relationships, achieve greater success at work, and lead more fulfilling lives. Take, for example, my client, Lucy, a team leader in a tech firm. Lucy was intelligent and skilled but often struggled with team conflicts. She had a habit of being reactive rather than responsive, which led to disagreements escalating into major problems.

When Lucy and I began working on improving her emotional intelligence, the first step was awareness. We used journaling as a tool to help her become more aware of her emotions. Each evening, she would reflect on her emotional state throughout the day, the triggers for any negative emotions, and how she responded to those feelings. Over time, Lucy began to recognize patterns and identify situations and factors that would cause emotional upheaval.

Next, we worked on emotional regulation. Techniques such as deep breathing, mindfulness, and progressive muscle relaxation proved beneficial for Lucy. We also explored cognitive restructuring – the practice of challenging and changing negative thought patterns. For instance, when Lucy found herself thinking, "I'll never be able to handle this team," we would work on reframing that thought to, "I can learn and improve my team management skills."

Improving emotional intelligence is not a quick process – it takes commitment, effort, and time. But it's worth it. As Lucy developed her emotional intelligence, her relationships with her team improved, conflicts reduced, and her overall job satisfaction increased significantly.

Emotional intelligence is flexible, meaning it can be developed. Regardless of where you are now, you can enhance your emotional intelligence and reap the benefits it offers for personal and professional success.

As a resource, I'd recommend the book "Emotional Intelligence 2.0" by Travis Bradberry and Jean Greaves. It's a practical guide that provides strategies for increasing emotional intelligence using the four core EQ skills: self-awareness, self-management, social awareness, and relationship management.

In conclusion, by nurturing your emotional intelligence, you can improve your ability to navigate the social complexities of the workplace, lead and motivate others, and excel in your career while also achieving a better balance in your personal life. Remember, it's not just about understanding your emotions but using them effectively to create a more harmonious and successful life.

# Chapter 4: Building Your Empire

# Cultivating Your Personal Brand

As we step into the first section of Chapter 4, "Building Your Empire," we traverse the exciting path of "Cultivating Your Personal Brand."

Imagine, if you will, the iconic brands in the world: Apple, Google, or even Oprah. The mere mention of their names invokes a specific image, a set of values, and a distinct emotional response. That's the power of a brand. Your personal brand carries the same significance in portraying who you are, what you stand for, and how you wish to be perceived by the world. It's not about creating a façade but about authentically and strategically presenting your true self to the world.

I've coached numerous individuals over the years who've strived to build their empires, and one thing that stood out was their unique personal brands. Let's look at Jason, a self-taught software engineer. He was skilled and hardworking but was having trouble standing out. His story was like that of many others, until we began to dig deeper into what made Jason unique.

Jason had a knack for making complex concepts seem simple. He also had a profound love for comic books. We combined these elements to develop his personal brand. Jason started a blog where he explained coding concepts through comic book metaphors. His unique approach got him noticed, and he quickly established a reputation as the "comic book coder."

Crafting your personal brand requires introspection. You have to understand what sets you apart from the crowd. Your unique experiences, your values, your passion – these are the elements that make up your personal brand. And keep in mind, your personal brand isn't set in stone. It can evolve as you grow and learn.

Building a personal brand involves being consistent with your message and image in every interaction you have, both online and offline. This consistency aids in reinforcing who you are and what you stand for. Whether it's the way you dress, how you communicate, your online presence, or the way you treat others – every element should be a reflection of your personal brand.

Tools such as a personal website, professional social media profiles, and even a blog can be used to showcase your personal brand. Remember, the goal is not to impress everyone, but to connect authentically with the audience that resonates with your brand.

To help in this journey, a resource I highly recommend is "Reinventing You: Define Your Brand, Imagine Your Future" by Dorie Clark. Clark provides a step-by-step guide on how to assess your unique strengths, develop a compelling personal brand, and ensure that others recognize the powerful contribution you can make.

Like a lighthouse guiding ships at sea, your personal brand helps others navigate toward you. It helps them understand who you are and what you represent. The work involved in cultivating your personal brand is, therefore, an investment in your future – a fundamental building block in creating your empire. In the end, your personal brand is about making your mark on the world – leaving a legacy that's uniquely and authentically yours.

# NETWORKING AND RELATIONSHIP BUILDINGS

As we delve deeper into the essence of building your empire, a compelling component that we encounter is the art of "Networking and Relationship Building." Success, in its entirety, isn't a solitary journey but a vibrant tapestry woven by the threads of relationships you foster along your path.

Let's look at Sarah, a fledgling entrepreneur I guided through her early years of business. In the beginning, like many others, Sarah focused on honing her craft and perfecting her product. Still, her business wasn't growing at the pace she'd hoped. It was when she turned her attention to networking and relationship building that her venture truly began to flourish.

Through her connections, Sarah found a mentor, secured investment, and gained valuable insights into her industry. Each relationship opened up a new opportunity, and soon her business was thriving.

The lesson from Sarah's story is that networking isn't about transactional relationships; it's about building meaningful connections that offer mutual value. When you approach networking from this perspective, you'll find that the process becomes more fulfilling and less daunting. Remember, it's not about how many business cards you can distribute at an event, but about the genuine connections you make.

Networking is a skill, and like any skill, it can be learned and refined. It starts with active listening. When you genuinely listen to what others are saying, it shows respect and interest. It allows you to understand their needs and how you can potentially add value.

The second aspect of effective networking is being open and approachable. This doesn't mean you have to be extroverted or the life of the party. It means being genuinely open to new ideas, perspectives, and people. Remember, the goal isn't to impress people but to connect with them authentically.

Another powerful networking tool is finding common ground, a shared interest, or a shared goal. Common ground acts as a bridge connecting you to another person, making your interactions more engaging and memorable.

As you nurture your network, don't forget about the power of follow-ups. A simple message expressing your appreciation for the conversation or sharing something of value related to your discussion can go a long way in fostering lasting relationships.

Building relationships requires time and consistent effort. It's about nurturing the connections you have made through thoughtful gestures, maintaining communication, and providing support when they need it.

Moreover, the dynamics of networking have significantly transformed in the digital age. Online platforms like LinkedIn, Twitter, and industry-specific forums offer vast opportunities for building professional relationships. They allow you to reach out to industry leaders, potential clients, or collaborators that would've been otherwise difficult to connect with.

As a reference for further improving your networking skills, I recommend reading "Never Eat Alone" by Keith Ferrazzi and Tahl Raz. This book is an excellent guide to networking for success in the modern world, filled with practical tips and techniques.

In the grand scheme of building your empire, networking and relationship building might seem like one piece of the puzzle. But it's a piece that connects other pieces together. It can open doors to opportunities, foster collaborations, bring in mentors, and provide access to resources that would have otherwise been inaccessible. As the saying goes, "Your network is your net worth."

# The Power of Social Media

Social media, once a playground for digital natives, has now transformed into a powerful tool that individuals and businesses alike can utilize to forge connections, promote their brands, and even catalyze social movements. As we delve into the heart of "Building Your Empire," let's harness "The Power of Social Media."

Reflect on the story of James, an artist who'd been honing his craft in obscurity. His tale pivoted when he started sharing his artwork on Instagram. Through consistent sharing and engagement with his followers, James' online presence grew. His art reached people across the globe, and he began selling his work to a wider audience, catapulting his career to new heights. His tale beautifully illustrates the transformative potential that social media holds.

Social media provides a stage where you can showcase your brand, connect with your audience, and create a community. It isn't merely about promoting your product or services but about building a narrative around your brand and engaging with your audience. Transparency, authenticity, and consistency are pivotal in this digital sphere.

Developing a social media strategy that aligns with your brand and goals is essential. Begin by identifying your target audience, understanding their preferences, and tailoring your content to cater to their interests. Aiming to provide value, whether through informative content, inspiring stories, or compelling visuals, is key to engaging your audience.

One of the most powerful aspects of social media is its potential for engagement. It allows for a two-way communication street, where your audience can directly interact with you. Encouraging this interaction by asking questions, initiating discussions, or requesting feedback can foster a sense of community around your brand.

Harnessing the power of social media is not without its challenges. With its fast-paced nature and constant evolution, staying relevant can sometimes seem like a Sisyphean task. However, flexibility, experimentation, and continuous learning are the tools to overcome these challenges.

Social media platforms are continually introducing new features such as Instagram Reels, LinkedIn Stories, and Facebook Live, among others. These present novel ways to reach and engage with your audience. Embrace these changes, experiment with these new features, and analyze what works best for your brand.

Keeping your mental wellbeing in check is equally essential as social media can sometimes be overwhelming. Allocate specific time for social media management and consider using tools that can automate the process.

For further insight into the power of social media, "Crushing It!: How Great Entrepreneurs Build Their Business and Influence—and How You Can, Too" by Gary Vaynerchuk provides a comprehensive guide. Vaynerchuk shares success stories of entrepreneurs who have harnessed the power of social media and provides practical advice on how you can do the same.

In the grand quest of building your empire, harnessing the power of social media is like wielding a modern-day Excalibur. It opens up a world of possibilities and opportunities, allowing you to reach and engage with your audience like never before. However, it requires strategic use, authenticity, and continuous engagement. Remember, it's not the tool, but the craftsman who wields it that makes the difference.

# FINANCIAL MASTERY

Journey with me into the realm of "Financial Mastery," an essential pillar in the architecture of your empire. Let's reflect on Sara's story, a brilliant entrepreneur whose ventures kept failing due to her limited financial acumen. However, once she embraced the pursuit of financial mastery, she not only revived her business but steered it towards uncharted heights of success. Her story is a testament to the crucial role of financial literacy in empire-building.

Managing your finances is not just about numbers, calculations, and spreadsheets. It's an intricate dance that combines discipline, foresight, patience, and strategy. It encompasses understanding where your money is coming from, where it's going, and making strategic decisions about its utilization to bolster your financial health.

In this pursuit, the first practical tool to wield is budgeting. By tracking income and expenditures, a budget becomes your financial roadmap, guiding your decisions and keeping you on track. It can spotlight areas of unnecessary spending, enabling you to direct your resources towards your financial goals.

Investing, a key element of financial mastery, is not just for the wealthy. It's a method to generate more income, preparing for future uncertainties, and building wealth over time. But remember, investing is a marathon, not a sprint. Start small, diversify your portfolio, and be patient.

Safeguarding your hard-earned assets is just as important. Insurance acts as a protective shield, mitigating risks associated with life's unpredictable nature. While it may seem like an unnecessary expenditure now, its value becomes evident when faced with a financial crisis.

As your financial mastery strengthens, the concept of debt will no longer be a source of anxiety but a strategic tool that can be used wisely to grow your empire. But caution must be exercised. Differentiating between good debt that generates value, like a business loan, and bad debt that diminishes value, such as high-interest credit cards, is crucial.

The journey to financial mastery is not devoid of pitfalls. Financial markets can be volatile, investments can fail, and financial decisions can backfire. It's important to have a contingency plan for such instances, ensuring your empire can withstand these financial storms.

One of the best practices for financial mastery is continuous learning. The world of finance is ever-evolving, with new investment options, financial instruments, and economic trends emerging. Books like "Rich Dad Poor Dad" by Robert Kiyosaki, "The Intelligent Investor" by Benjamin Graham, and "Think and Grow Rich" by Napoleon Hill provide timeless advice on financial literacy and wealth creation.

Remember, there is no one-size-fits-all approach to financial mastery. It varies based on individual goals, risk tolerance, and circumstances. Flexibility in adapting your financial strategies to align with your changing needs and economic conditions is a vital aspect of this journey.

In essence, financial mastery goes beyond making money. It's about making your money work for you, safeguarding your assets, preparing for uncertainties, and ultimately steering you towards financial freedom. It's an ongoing journey filled with learning, adaptation, and growth, leading not only to the construction of your empire but also to its preservation and expansion.

# Chapter 5: Celebrating the Journey

# EMBRACING YOUR ACHIEVEMENTS

The narrative now brings us to the heartwarming phase of "Embracing Your Achievements." The concept takes root from the wisdom of my late grandmother, who always found joy in every small victory. Through her lens, I began to realize that our life is a grand tapestry woven with threads of numerous victories, some large, some small, but each significant in shaping our journey.

Life's journey is like climbing a mountain. The summit, often symbolizing our ultimate goal, can only be reached by overcoming countless smaller peaks. It is those smaller victories, those intermediate peaks that fuel our ascent towards the ultimate summit. By embracing these victories, we feed our spirit with positivity, fortitude, and motivation.

This brings us to our first tool: A Victory Journal. The purpose of this journal is to document your achievements, no matter how small. Jotting down these moments of success serves to boost your morale and provides a source of inspiration during challenging times. It's a testament to your capabilities, showcasing how far you have come.

Every success story, be it Bill Gates or Oprah Winfrey, was punctuated with milestones - both big and small. These milestones weren't just progress markers, but they were also moments of self-recognition and celebration. Gates didn't wait to become the richest man in the world to start celebrating. He savored the joy of his first successful code, his first client, the launch of Microsoft, and so forth. These celebrations fueled his journey forward.

Recognition from self and others plays a crucial role in human motivation. One key to embracing your achievements is sharing your successes with others, your loved ones, or your community. It allows for external validation, appreciation, and creates a positive feedback loop that spurs further achievement.

Just as we embrace our achievements, we must also honor our journey. Each step, each stumble, each triumph, and each setback is a part of our story. Adopt the practice of regular reflection. Reflect not only on the end result but on the path you traversed to get there - the courage you showed, the obstacles you overcame, and the resilience you exhibited.

And while we bask in the glow of our achievements, let us not forget to extend our gratitude. Gratitude to the universe for providing opportunities, gratitude to our loved ones for their unwavering support, and most importantly, gratitude to ourselves for our relentless pursuit.

However, remember that embracing your achievements should not become an obsession with perfection or an avenue for comparison. It should be a personal journey, an acknowledgment of your efforts and progress. Embracing achievements is not a destination, but a journey of continuous growth and self-recognition.

Let's also debunk the myth that embracing achievements equates to complacency. Quite the contrary, it fuels ambition. Celebrating a victory doesn't mean we stop striving; instead, it amplifies our appetite for success.

In terms of resources, books such as "The Power of Now" by Eckhart Tolle and "Daring Greatly" by Brene Brown, can offer profound insights into the art of living in the moment and embracing victories.

In conclusion, life is a symphony composed of various notes, each representing a moment, an effort, a victory. By embracing our achievements, we're honoring the symphony of our lives. As we move forward, let's carry this perspective in our hearts: Every step we take is an achievement in its own right. Every effort we put forth is a testament to our spirit. And every goal we reach is a celebration of our journey. So let's embrace our achievements, for they are the melodies that compose the symphony of our lives.

# Reflecting and Adjusting

As we continue our journey through life, we embark on the road of "Reflecting and Adjusting". This stage is just as important as setting goals or celebrating victories because it's where growth and learning are fostered. It is where we assess our path, look back at the roads traveled, and chart the course for the roads yet to be explored.

Imagine sailing across the ocean. Without stopping to check the compass or adjusting the sails, one can easily be driven off course. Our lives are much like that journey, and reflection serves as our compass, while adjustment acts as the steering wheel guiding our ship on the course to success.

A personal story comes to mind: When I first started my career as a life coach, there were moments of doubt and confusion. I was new to the field, constantly comparing my journey with those who had years of experience. But it was through reflection that I found my path. I looked back at my journey, acknowledging my passion and desire to help others, and my unique perspective shaped by my experiences. Through reflection, I was able to understand my strengths and adjust my approach to coaching, allowing me to bring my unique self to the profession and serve my clients better.

The cornerstone of reflection and adjustment is the practice of mindfulness, a state of active, open attention on the present. This powerful tool allows us to understand our thoughts, feelings, and actions at a deeper level. Mindfulness enables us to evaluate our decisions, behaviors, and outcomes critically, providing the foundation for meaningful reflection and effective adjustment.

One way to harness mindfulness is through the practice of meditation. It helps you understand your mind better, enabling you to become an impartial observer of your thoughts and feelings. This unbiased self-observation aids in deep reflection and fosters a greater ability to adjust.

Adjustment is the natural progression from reflection. It entails making changes based on our reflections to better align with our goals and aspirations. It could mean tweaking our approach, altering our mindset, or changing our direction altogether.

The concept of Kaizen, a Japanese philosophy of continuous improvement, holds valuable insights for this stage of the journey. Kaizen encourages small, incremental changes over time, leading to substantial growth and improvement. So, don't feel pressured to make big, radical adjustments. Even a minor course correction can lead you to a significantly different destination over time.

A recommended resource to aid your journey is the book "Mindfulness: An Eight-Week Plan for Finding Peace in a Frantic World" by Mark Williams and Danny Penman. This book provides practical steps to incorporate mindfulness into your everyday life, helping you cultivate a habit of reflection.

As we conclude this section, remember that the road to success is not always a straight path. It's a winding road filled with twists, turns, ups, and downs. Through reflection, we learn from our journey, and through adjustment, we continue to grow and move forward. Keep reflecting, keep adjusting, and keep moving forward on this incredible journey of life.

# The Art of Gratitude

Our journey through life is filled with numerous peaks and valleys. It's a beautiful tapestry of experiences that shape who we are and what we become. Throughout this journey, one quality stands out as a beacon of hope and source of strength: the art of gratitude.

The art of gratitude is the practice of acknowledging and appreciating the positives in our life. It's about focusing on what's going well, what's working, and what brings us joy. It's about finding the silver lining in every cloud, no matter how dark.

Take a moment to reflect on your life. There are so many things we often take for granted. The warmth of the sun on our skin, the love and support of our friends and family, the fact that we woke up today, the opportunities and challenges that help us grow - all these deserve our gratitude.

I remember a time in my life when things were not going well. I had lost my job, and the future seemed uncertain. It was during this challenging period that I stumbled upon the transformative power of gratitude. By shifting my focus to what I had rather than what I lacked, I was able to navigate through the stormy seas of uncertainty with a sense of optimism and hope.

Expressing gratitude is not just about making a list of things we're thankful for, although that's a great place to start. It's about embodying a mindset of appreciation and allowing it to permeate every aspect of our lives. It's about noticing the small things, expressing thanks for the big things, and appreciating everything in between.

One practical technique to harness the power of gratitude is through the practice of keeping a gratitude journal. Every day, write down three things you're grateful for. They don't have to be grand or profound - even the simplest things count. Over time, this practice can shift your mindset and help you focus on the abundance in your life, rather than the lack.

Another technique is the "Gratitude Walk". This involves taking a leisurely walk and consciously looking for things to be grateful for. It could be the beauty of nature, the laughter of children playing, or the comfort of a warm breeze.

One resource I recommend for further exploration is "The Magic" by Rhonda Byrne. This book offers a deeper understanding of the power and practice of gratitude, along with practical exercises to enhance your practice.

Remember, gratitude is more than just saying "thank you". It's a way of seeing the world, a way of life. It doesn't mean ignoring the challenges or difficulties in life, but it does mean choosing to focus on the good and finding reasons to be thankful in every situation. As we continue to celebrate our journey through life, let us carry with us the art of gratitude. After all, it's not happiness that brings us gratitude. It's gratitude that brings us happiness.

# Savoring the Moment

In this beautiful journey of life, filled with ups and downs, twists and turns, there is one practice that can profoundly enrich our experience: savoring the moment. As we forge ahead, driven by our goals, it's easy to get lost in the flurry of activities and forget to enjoy the beauty of the present. So let's embark on an exploration of what it means to savor the moment, and how we can infuse this practice into our lives.

We live in a society that encourages constant movement, constant doing. This has led many of us to get so caught up in the doing that we forget about the being. We're always planning for the future, reminiscing about the past, and in the process, we lose sight of the present. And yet, it's the present moment that holds the key to our joy and satisfaction. This is where savoring comes in.

Savoring is the practice of stepping out of the normal flow of time to appreciate and enjoy a positive experience. It's about extracting the maximum possible satisfaction from an experience while it's happening, and even after it's passed. Savoring intensifies and lengthens our positive emotions, giving us more bang for our emotional buck, so to speak.

There are many ways to savor, and each person might find different methods that work best for them. However, some strategies are widely applicable and have been validated by research. These include sharing the experience with others, taking mental photographs, expressing gratitude for the experience, and focusing on the sensory details.

Think back to a time when you experienced a deep sense of joy, peace, or satisfaction. Maybe it was while you were watching a beautiful sunset, spending time with a loved one, or achieving a long-desired goal. Now think about how you can slow down during these moments to truly savor them. How would that deepen your experience of joy, peace, and satisfaction?

One way to practice savoring is by doing a daily 'savoring walk'. This is a leisurely stroll where your goal is to appreciate the sights, sounds, and smells around you. As you walk, try to stay present and focus on the sensory details. What do you see? What do you hear? What do you smell? How does the air feel on your skin?

Another practical tool is the 'three good things' exercise. Every day, write down three good things that happened and how they made you feel. This encourages you to not only notice positive events but to savor them.

In the book "Savoring: A New Model of Positive Experience", authors Fred B. Bryant and Joseph Veroff offer an in-depth look at savoring, its benefits, and how to cultivate it. It's a valuable resource for anyone looking to enrich their experience of life.

Let's embrace the power of savoring the moment. The journey of life is not a race to the finish line, but a dance to be enjoyed in every step. By slowing down, paying attention, and reveling in the here and now, we can infuse our lives with a sense of richness and joy that's available to us in every moment. After all, the past is history, the future is a mystery, but the present is a gift. That's why it's called the present.

www.ingramcontent.com/pod-product-compliance
Lightning Source LLC
Chambersburg PA
CBHW071253070526
44583CB00017B/2454